Far-
Flung

Far-Flung

Rhian Gallagher

AUCKLAND
UNIVERSITY
PRESS

First published 2020
Auckland University Press
University of Auckland
Private Bag 92019
Auckland 1142
New Zealand
www.press.auckland.ac.nz

ISBN 978 1 86940 911 1

Published with the assistance of Creative New Zealand

ARTS COUNCIL OF NEW ZEALAND TOI AOTEAROA

A catalogue record for this book is available from the
National Library of New Zealand

This book was printed on FSC® certified paper

Designed by Greg Simpson
Printed in Singapore by Markono Print Media Pte Ltd

Inside cover: Detail of topographical map showing Dunedin and vicinity
[cartographic material] / from surveys by W. T. Neill, district surveyor;
R. T. Sadd, chief surveyor, Otago; M. Crompton-Smith, chief draughtsman.
Ref: 834.52cba 1922. Alexander Turnbull Library, Wellington, New Zealand.

for Jane Duran & Alison Rutherford

Contents

THE SPEED OF GOD

SEACLIFF EPISTLES

The Speed of God

Into the Blue Light

for Kate Vercoe

I'm walking above myself in the blue light
indecently blue above the bay with its walk-on-water skin
here is the Kilmog slumping seaward
and the men in their high-vis vests
pouring tar and metal on gaping wounds
the last repair broke free; the highway
doesn't want to lie still, none of us
want to be where we are

exactly but somewhere else
the track a tree's ascent, kaikawaka! hold on
to the growing power, sun igniting little shouts
against my eyeballs
and clouds come from Australia
hunkering over the Tasman with their strange accent

I'm high as a wing tip
where the ache meets the bliss
summit rocks exploding with lichen and moss –
little soft fellas suckered to a groove
bloom and bloom – the track isn't content
with an end, flax rattling their sabres, tussocks
drying their hair in the stiff south-easterly;
                    the track wants to go on
forever because it comes to nothing
but the blue light. I'm going out, out
out into the blue light, walking above myself.

The Speed of God

What if God slowed down after making the grass and the
stars and the whales and let things settle for a bit so the day
could practise leaving into the arms of the night and the
tides tinker their rhythms and the stars
find their most dramatic positions.

Or maybe if he'd made man and said, 'You learn how to
live with yourself and do housework and then I might think
about woman.'

Or instead he'd made woman not out of a rib, which was
really such a last resort, but rising out of the firmament one
woman followed by more women and they took journeys
and learnt how to build boats and bridges which surely they
would have done without men around pushing and shoving
and constantly giving orders.

I just think it was a bit fast – six days to make all of it. How
could the relationship between things be seen, be felt?

And as if God's rush were in us too we go about remodelling
faster and faster with our burning and breaking and the earth
reels with our speed and it looks and feels like a disaster.

Titipounamu Tapping the Beech Forest

for Laurence Fearnley

Our smallest bird, a visionary speck
in the cool, calm, cathedral-quiet of the beech forest;
the milk-moss, fern-fanned floor
where I lie down and wait

hearing a million tiny rhizoid voices, the high-up canopy
consorting with the sun, light
falling through a found gap
makes music with the moist green, gem

to gem. Above my eye comes titipounamu
on the trunk that hasn't opened yet – once more
she scales the rough-ridged bark
tap-tap, wing flick, tap-tap-tap she looks up

to see what's happened in the last three seconds
then back to the tree: *bow, swivel, tap-tap-tap*
as if she will find the key one day – open
and open – all of the secrets of the beech forest
                        bursting free.

Huxley Valley

Moth

Courier of bloom powder
the river meadow agog with flower head;
low-lying daisy wakes with the sun and turns
till dark hushes each petal and all the hubbub dies down.
Even sandfly, vampire of the light, gives up
his head-butting crawl across glass while moth
is up all hours with her deliveries.

Streamcut

River bucks and veers
taking the boulders at a glance
– I am a child of the river
small in my parts and barely audible

yet I too may grow into a bed of gallons
under the sway of sky
overnight, the rain like breath
filling my body till I roar

and you can say
you knew me
when I was only a trickle.

Mackenzie Country

Tucked into snow tussock's span
shy gentian – *one life holding another* –
did butterfly consent
to draw her wings closed? come October
mountain daisy
rose like an earth-sun, orchid
peeked from its cover

the bracts and the berries and the leaves
wetlands' quiet webbing
the watery sails of spider-work
banqueting bees without a flower

did midge and fly consent
to the clot and clog of the flow?
Ahuriri-Hakataramea-Waitaki-Tekapo
the river soul slips from the fish
perishing, the land soul

slips – a plenitude
narrowed and yoked
the weave unpicked
and the stitch – nothing

but the great loneliness
            of grass.

Learning to Read

Your friends progress
writing their stories. Sunlight peers
through motes of chalk.
This is your timeless time. The alphabet
lives on the blackboard's top line
– each letter has a big brother
or a big sister.

Miss Breen can see
there's some far place in you.
Fantail stutters from the window tree.
You stand beside the island of her desk.
Your friends are busy; even the tadpoles
are working themselves
out and into frogs.

You can't tell what you see
– the words are shapes
and the schoolroom's paused.
Bright crayonned houses
pinned to the wall; the piano waiting
to be woken with a touch.
All of the doors that will open.

Her finger steers
crossing the page – you tilt
your voice in reply; through your held-back days
you are her echo.
The smell of Miss Breen. The story
is everything.

Home

A whereabouts that grew
out of two miles and a nor'west wind
that fortune made   mattered
less in my doing days
managed like a high-wire walker
being in two places
at one time   earthed and above
here and away   how the soul
works against gravity   yet
tied to the body   a string of code
'Nothing but pinex board and timber,'
my brother says
'the whole place could have gone up
at the drop of a hat.'

◆ ◆ ◆

A worn hollow   my favourite seat
the backdoor step   her work shuffle
in the kitchen behind   blade on the board
clattering across carrots like heels on pavement
the line to the house
as I go out   (my homework done)
a song line   spirit line   the little air bubble
balanced between my eyebrows
as I press down on the barbwire top-rung of the fence
and jump

into the next province   the line
that would come as I go   an invisible road
into the next country   into the next world
it would hold.

Normanby

As if the night had lost its way
and the sun might never set
the crop kicks up its heels and it feels like forever
and forever and the combine harvester
sounds out on the townland edge – stalks
scooped up in the threshing, grain
shaking down a chute – and a dust cloud
rolls in the wake and the gulls agitate
and the small birds follow in the flung seed-spree.

10th April 1968

We're cutting through the paddocks for home
as the wind grows, it grows
like an animal, our voices drown in the roar.
Clods fly up from their bed, the little kids
are scared, we try to keep our heads
above the air, a sheep lorry goes past on a lean
then my dad swoops in from nowhere
pulling me out of the wind, 'thank God' he says.

♦ ♦ ♦

The wind keeps coming for more, the shed roof
sails over the lawn, everywhere is drag and claw,
it feels like the house might surrender.
The transistor voice is our centre, the ferry
is the size of a field. 'These night prayers,'
mum says, 'are given up for the rescue.'
But isn't God steering the storm?
A horn blows, a judder, behind the window
where I lie, the waves breaking into my dreams. The sea
will never be the same.

The Illuminated Page

The afternoon released   last class   freed
from the sentence of a sentence   to dawdle out
along a shingle verge   the heady scent
of gum trees in the gully   changing pace
as magpies swoop down from their watchtower

to outrun time and enter space
– the unsupervised, unscripted primer –
dry grasses   a dust-caked hum
the riddle of the creek-bed   dragonflies and reeds
a wilding apple sharp upon my tongue.

Before home   and the night descending
to rhyme my way across a wheat field   floating
on the plains' big sky   inland gulls like envoys
their telegraphic cries that said *not far to go* . . .
not far to go became a day   a moment

in a single hour   words woke upon the page
sense with sense converged   shapes
became a sound I made   to suffer
the illumination   gain set on the scales
with loss   the world forever after in translation.

Kōtukutuku

I take my bearings from the stream below
tree or not tree
I bow above the waterflow

terracotta, ochre, subtle rose
my bark enacts the light
in this country of so many greens

the record of myself I wear
– a ragged bride, her train in tatters –
I make my fluid stride, letting go

and partly shredded
I look like a historical document
unresolved, I grow.

Country Hall

Bring-a-plate occasions, flagon beer,
rites of passage: final year
school concert, a twenty-first, the wedding dance
– moths scaling up the entrance glass
bar heaters coughing into life

the get-up and the let-down
awkward in suits, immaculate hair-dos

the gravel spit of car park where the lights left off
a stage for fist fights – men
with a skinful, gone berserk; and the dangerous
liaisons in the car-room, backseat bedsits

those simple-complex nights – the hall
lit up like a liner
in a sea of paddocks; the country dark
turning stars into an anthem
warbling and symphonic.

Kāhu

she could break from her ease and drop into a dive

every small whim of the wind
she adjusts to
riffling feathers
rapids of air
in which she excels

was it the sky that hatched her?

finger-feathered salute
her spiralled ascent on the slope updraft of Mt Charlotte
my eye in pursuit
Kāhu, the victor,
homing the high space

she disappears through the top of the picture.

Laced in with the Wind

What did the wind want with the house
muttering? below on the flat
stillness or something close to a breeze;
cresting the hill my bike at an angle
or the settling-in of an hour
noised-up with the whistling eaves. Roses
hollowed their heads on the worked-up air
the backyard birch bowed
like a monk at penance, and those small hopeful trees
you set in a splint – strapped to a stake
as if the break had already happened.

          Birds flustered to wrong flying
          guttered down the chimney into the firebox
          – one saved, one too late to free:
          ghastly, unintended

what was the wind asking us –
our share, under the same roof, the *us* of us
unspeaking speech?
Days when it gave us a breather, days
when the hills were at their best and an old calm
wandered down the hallway; we could leave
the doors open and not miss each other.

Wooden Horse

for Becky Cameron

That day I came round
to pick up last things
– books that had merged
with yours on the shelves
and the small wooden horse
with a broken leg and broken hoof,
you asked
did it mean something to me?

for a moment we poised in the question's sway
till our eyes gave way
and finding your kit, the glue and small instruments,
you sat at the kitchen table
with that open concentration
that could keep you on a hillside
sketching for hours.

           I'd picked him up from a pavement stash
           outside a junk shop on a London street
           – chipped and weathered, a gallant prance

travelling in time
as I watched you make the repair
with fix and adjust
and what more

could be found in a moment's exchange:
the small wooden horse
back on his feet – we too
had changed.

It's Strange the Way That Memory

loses laughter, dilutes the larger part
of joy and play
and bends the truth of wonder
yet never hesitates, at 3am,
to detail and exact
the hardest time, the roughest weather
our worst fight ever, the jolts
of fear.

Salt Marsh

Though I can't see beyond the entrance
there's a honeycomb of housing below
past crab burrow to ghost shrimp and worm

sparking in the wet
catacombs of vitality, so busy down there,
small mouths on which this world leans.

◆　◆　◆

What the body might feel
before thought: to inhabit skin
as a girl can, without meaning to.

Provisional, perishing, not solid ground
crossing the saltwort meadow
fossicking the ragged seam:

cast and carapace, small bird bones
a floating harvest of eelgrass –
weed pasted in like a poultice.

◆　◆　◆

I've walked the salt marsh in sunlight
come back in the depths of night
to listen to geese at their pillow talk

the moon holding on to what it can't have
brings the sea to my ear; a boundary found
then lost again – on this waterlogged map
my whereabouts is 'almost' or 'maybe'.

Small Bird without a Sky

She flew in through an open door
– what can I hear from her?
corralled inside the corridor
where nothing works as once it did

the shrinking space, the disbelief
where each week I take
again the thinking cure
'think not these thoughts'

when asked
to chart my progress
I hover on the brink
of 1–10 *and think and think*

how the sky became a lid
walls she has no map for;
the window replies with tree
and cloud, she flutters up against

the hope, the doubt.
Feather unto skin, creature
to creature, a message being sent:
how a search begins

– this rapid, rapid beating.

Tears, Trees, Birds & Grass

for Maia Mistral

I sit down under the dawn redwood tree and cry
and cry. After a time I think, 'OK, that's enough tears'
but there are always more, a tear-rain
falling, raining – I am turning
into the country of Ireland.

I look at the dawn redwood tree
Maia says it is a living fossil.

Maia is away. She is on Stewart Island looking for kiwi.
She has lent me the old school-house library

inside the library there is a table, a chair, a bed
an armchair and a wood-burning stove.
On the floor there is a bag of books
– I am pretending to be a writer. I lie on the floor
pretending to be a writer. I sit at the table
this is more difficult

the door is open. The outside is nearby.
The birds come and go.

I wonder if a bird ever wakes up in the morning
sick with the business of singing.
Do the birds cry? I have never seen them cry.
Maybe they do it when I'm not looking.

Maia returns every two weeks or so.
As soon as I see her I start to cry. I have forgotten
how to be around human beings.
My words have turned into water

could this miracle continue
and the water turn into wine and the wine
turn back into words. . . .
When I am not planting a tear-garden
under the dawn redwood tree
or pretending to be a writer,
I am mowing the grass.

Maia has lots of grass.
'Maia,' I say, 'you have too much grass.'
'I know,' she says, 'but now I've got it under control
I want to keep it that way.'

The garden is not under control
but the mowed grass
makes it seem like it could be soon.

I start with the top patch of grass
which is a long way away from the library.
I drag the mower behind me
through the small gate
up the narrow tree-lined track.
The mower and I
grapple with each other among the tree roots

up, up to the kidney-shaped bit of grass
at the top. I pull on the cord of the mower.
It always takes more than one pull
then there is that satisfying pull
followed by a big noise

though sometimes I resent the mower.
'It's OK for you,' I say, 'being a machine,
all I have to do is pull on your cord
and eventually you break into life.
You want to try being a human being.'

I have to stop talking to the mower.

Sometimes everything happens at once:
mowing, crying, pretending to be a writer

and I push the mower
into the rough scrubby bit
and choke it to death.

Maybe this is why the birds don't seem to cry
– flying with tears in their eyes would not be safe.

I mow for an hour or so. I don't really know
how long I mow for.
The hours have gone from the day; there are no more hours

there is only the light and the dark.

The Old Cemetery

it is like the sun going down

when I walk through the tall iron gates
atmosphere folds
to a moss and lichen era; headstones
holding onto their names, softly
avalanching –

is it that gravity is more intense here?

in the old cemetery I could not skip or dance
if I tried; each step goes
life-death, life-death
trees and birds
become rafts in the swirling tides

and the feeling, as in a church or a temple,
that something is being asked of me
I do not know
what is being asked of me –
I find myself listening intently

– generations after
memory thins to a sound
beyond the human ear

leaving behind
the old cemetery, the permanent residents
the beauty, the apprehension.

The Year Between

It was the year between before and after,
God slept in the roots of the plane trees,
the horizon was talked of
but I couldn't find it.
My country was going away.

There were the last of the waves –
my mother's hand, my father's hand
where all the events were recorded
like music wrought in the wind.

It was the year of myself walking into myself
and walking back out again.
A chestnut shone, an autumn leaf
and how their deaths returned me
bent to a grave as if looking into a mirror.

Triptych

for Jane Duran

August Snow

The long straight roads
crossing the plains, fences
staking the distance, a distance
that has never been straight –
the way back or the way to
– horizons open and close, open and close,
the wipers swing snow drift from the screen.

Softening lines, freighting the windbreak trees;
a musky earth-scent not yet risen –
the wide openness I drive out into
the where to live, how to live.

While the Light Lasts

To reach the small town
while the light lasts
before the freeze
sets black ice on the road
or a stag, driven down
from its high place
by hunger, looms
in the headlight and I'm
too late

not to mistake
freedom for safety
as the dark
marries into the land
nothing to withstand it
– the going, the gone.

The Roost Trees

Two shaggy old macrocarpas
break into morning song, the birds
having sheltered the night freeze
one body to another in a hug of green;
come spring, they will claim their territories
but we're not there yet.

The big red mail truck out on its rounds
travelling miles between houses
and as if harsh weather worked like a burnish
the sky freshly minted, the pitched roofs glitter
facets of snow with the spark of opal.

It's this southern light that knows me
I can't hide in the gaze of it
though I'm claimed by the distance
– leaving home long enough to be a stranger
sets a yearning in motion

while those who stay
never think of home
                    imagine
a morning like this between seasons
exposed as the ridge line in the west
and across that span to meet halfway

the roost trees breasting with call,
call and response – hurry
with a kind of happiness, a coming
round, a coming to.

At the Boatshed

for Sonja Mitchell

We carried the day through the door
the harbour had earned its keep
light laid its hands on each contour

the shed held abreast with the shore
spreading the waves in pleats
we carried the day through the door

tide played a rift to the floor
retreat and return, it was speaking
as light laid its hands on each contour

the reds and the greens and the blues in rapport
lines apart and meeting
we carried the day through the door

time was like something we wore
shedding, left a wide scope in its wake
the day with its openings, the door,
light laying hands on each contour.

Short Takes on My Father

The boy bottled up inside him
wrote Irish for the short days of his schooling
his sister called him 'the scholar',
the rest of his life
was a great unlearning.

♦   ♦   ♦

Great Grandmother raised him.
Heather and stone, a struggling field
headland like an arm in the sea
– a brooding ground
that tied his tongue.

♦   ♦   ♦

As if there were a mile to each word
my mother said, 'He still had a long way to go
when he arrived here'

how far his distance was
I could only imagine, until
I went back the way he came.

♦   ♦   ♦

Sometimes he couldn't find a word
to save himself and screwed up
his fists between his knees
as if his arms held on to a signal.

♦   ♦   ♦

When he raised the spirit to his lips
and the music stirred
he would enter a private mist
removing his glasses, grinding
his eyes with his fist.

Descent

Dear Donegal, how you lived in my head –
fairy places, leprechaun interventions, the mystical
sad eyes of a donkey; curse of the English

and Kitty, great grandmother
calling from nowhere to nowhere.
Her portrait wore me out:

noble peasant, spiritual vessel
one among the apes. Or what
Yeats, Kavanagh or Synge made of her

what I had in my head
straying into her field, cattle treading puddles
to a mud pool. The dirt floor. The cottage ruins

all over Donegal women clattering their needles
click-clicking like instruments
their bodies swayed to the beat

knitting for pin money, after a day's toil,
an early version of nightshift, as cleaners
crossing pre-dawn streets to executive suites. Invisible.

She lived on in the clachan
between the asylum and the parish chapel, between
the workhouse and the grave

tales, half-truths, rumours and prayer
I foraged, home-coming among the ruins
– bog cotton, asphodel and ling, the view
sweeping out to the Atlantic. A line of descent.

Amanuensis

Words plucked and plaited into lines
for a loved one to unravel, dear hand
receive what's given, mirroring
as true as can be done, by composition
words made fit for travel.

A thousand laughs, a thousand tears, have fed
the living kitchen table – a pitted, polished
sounding board for 'was' and 'is'
and 'what's to come' – the speaker
in more minds than one.

With all the tenses aired, the spirit
of the letter waving at the door,
your task done – in this communal barter
hand to hand, hand to mouth –
a score of hens' eggs in your basket.

Seacliff Epistles

The only true madness is loneliness,
the monotonous voice in the skull
that never stops
because never heard

— John Montague, 'The Wild Dog Rose'

Epistle of Maeve

Isn't it queer how things come out? If only we knew what
was down the road . . . you marryin an opportunity (God
rest his soul) & me up here in the attic room pen in me hand,
thinkin me thoughts like & talkin with you

them church ladies praisin me efforts 'turning over a new
leaf,' they says, but it's just the same tree in the end. Sure
enough, up on the hill with the law-di-daws, the man of the
house eying me left, right & centre – him with his gropin,
slobberin ways

our days in the kiphouse was an honest living. Here it's all
pretendin one thing when it's another. . . .

You was askin after Agnes now, it's a bad turn she be havin,
she's after being sent to the madhouse. What I be thinkin,
there but for the grace of God . . . she kept grievin for her
boy, worn out with the troubles & no anchor

was there ever a world fit for our livin!

First Epistle of Grace

Each word I write is but a longing

. . . remembering our last hours together
out on the strand talking over our plans,
touching as if fragile and newly made

they say
I ought not to love you
that I am throwing my life away

there is nothing to be done.

I leave my country, my friends, the world of my girlhood

believing & hoping & believing

in what we are now, in what we may
become.

What You Knew about Water

It soaked in the bed of the turf
shone on the toe of the spade
the font was a holy wet
and there was a holy well
the small lake was an eye to the sky.
Water came down from above, you knew,
came down on the head of a child
you were that child in a shift.
Mixed with the spirit and drunk
in a toast, mixed with the air
made a mist and that was the face
of the Holy Ghost. You were born
in the land of the rain, rain
in so many forms: the buckets
the pours, the pelts, the soft and the dark
and the beautiful light left
like a halo on earth
when everything shone with a spark.
Yet nothing you knew about water
prepared you for the depth and the breadth
of the sea. The sea was a thing
apart. It was a great separator.

A Slip of a Girl

Agnes

The dance
rising to ecstasy

when the chasm
opened

sighted like quarry
falseness on his breath

he called you away
into the darkness

to be left
in a field

in the rain
split like a flower.

My Career

Agnes

God spoke through a priest
talking as if I were on the other side
of a thick wall – mud I would bring
to my father's name

so began my wilding
I went on the roads, I carried
the shame of it, *the women
I come from carried the Fall*
these things were happening

my fate in the hands of the powers
that be – my eyes & arms *animal*,
my hair & mouth *animal* – shipped
from the workhouse, wretched
a young beast in a shawl . . .

The Sea Road

Stem to stern, gull to gull crying *away*
– six hours rising, six hours
falling – the seven oceans and the many seas

    ◆ ◆ ◆

trying-your-luck
chancing-your-arm
everything-lost
so-nothing-to-lose. Some
didn't mean
to go so far, some
didn't choose but were sent

    ◆ ◆ ◆

hollow-eyed   in the swell
the unrelenting waves
home and sea   the sickness

    ◆ ◆ ◆

lying out there
between what's gone
and what's to come

◆　◆　◆

turning and turning
boundless, infinite, encircling
around the border of the world   who knows
if you ever won home.

'A Great Many Never Seen a Ship Before'

'Most of the passengers was South of Ireland the roughest
& worst class of people I am sure ever come here before &
nearly all R.C. If you had only heard them prayin when they
thought they were in danger when she used to be rolling
about. All the crowd that belong to her said they never
sailed in one lurched so much. There was a great many
never seen a ship before till they left Ireland & they were
in the greatest state if there was a sea come over her. Ever
you seen prayin to the Holy Mother & all other Half way
substitutes & next day if she ran steady [erased: illegible] like
came dancing & singing & cursing & swearing . . . '

A Luckless Birth

Agnes's son

The ship was a totem of no-hope mother
and you were the crest I fell from,
roped in your slipway, coming

head first into the world.
I heard the storm on the inside
then I entered it full tilt; you

stretched out on the pallet
submerged as I breached
into a dream of daylight.

You were a child
giving birth to a child, I was your son
for a moment . . . then

a man lowered his voice in prayer
the block swung, the board tilted
the waters opened.

Vacancy

Grace

She shaped what she could from the earth
– spuds and greens – shored up with a stock of firewood,
boiling water from a stream
on the edge of the city
each foot above sea level a foot above poverty.

'Not long to wait,' he wrote – news of gold
and drowning and fire-death.
And then nothing . . . her days descended to a rote
scoured out like a lone tree on stumpy ground
'this space cannot hear me,' she thought.

Cold came up through the thin foundations, six months in
she sleepwalked among the dwindling supplies
– silence from him. Eight months in
she pawned her wedding ring,
carried a nation on her back: THE IRISH NEED NOT APPLY.

Mean Time

I

Limbo's not a verb – between paradise
and burning – the only sound that's heard there
is an infant's cry.

II

Who waits for news waits on the edge
of time, hands weaving and unweaving

the fish rise, the sky clears
lovers love to wait, be it so, until

anticipation dies. Dead letter
holding pen – the mean time.

The Workhouse Girls

1874

Never having been
as far as the town of Belfast,
you land in Dunedin like cargo
filling a shortfall in the ship's quota

– a workhouse surplus

there were so many
of your people
in the workhouse
the guardians
gave up on plates
& introduced feeding troughs.

♦   ♦   ♦

Memory Serves You Well

When a road's verge
became a garden,
roots and stalks, to tuck in
to the shame of it

you carried that value
to this far place

what nothing to nothing
could teach:

a meal
and a freight of hunger
bent to the plate, one mouthful
amazed by another

not to pause or race, not to tear
like scavenging dog,
a scrap could be lost
in your haste.

◆　◆　◆

The workhouse came with you, though you left it behind,
it was in your hair, in your voices. It was in your clothes,
what clothes you had. It was Irish, Irish, Irish

you were re-baptised
in the name of the workhouse
you were named

blight, certified scum, parasitical organisms

◆　◆　◆

the wild Irish workhouse girls
arriving at a time

when everything wild
was being tamed,

the country was to be flooded with light.

The bush, wild & full of shadows,
was being tamed. The swamps
where dark earth met the welling water, the swamps,
which few seem to have actually looked at,
were drained, dried, burnt

in a country being flooded with light
there was no place for shadow.
That there could have been shadows
in the souls of the good colonists was unthinkable
for there was so much work to be done

all their contending energies, urges, impulses, desires, fears
were placed outside where the outsiders lived

& this is how
the workhouse girls – lazy, unemployed,
deviant, drunken, parasitical,
worthless workhouse girls –

became the bearers
of the shadows in the souls of the good colonists
& were sentenced to hard labour.

◆　◆　◆

Your Many, Many Crimes

You were robbing honey from a hive of bees
out in the country and at the same time
pouncing on men in Walker Street
making them drunk, taking advantage

you could be in three places at once
with the bees and the men and yet houses away
stealing clothes from a line
– you were like atomic particles.

Fleet

Agnes and Maeve and Deirdre
in joy, in sorrow, in everything
an unholy trinity.

When your ways parted
– powerless
and about to be tamed – Deirdre

topped the wall like a bird
and fled for her life
from the Salvationists.

◆   ◆   ◆

Shouting oaths, having words,
raw-boned, quick-tongued, not petticoats
& needlework, not sweet-voiced & invisible, not
anchored with fathers, brothers, husbands,
not stay-put
put up with anything
women, not heroine pioneers

but perplexed, peripheral, raging

        the wild Irish workhouse girls.

Riddle

I'm the tooth in the hair-triggered trap
the hone against steel
heat in a claw, I'm the barb
sewn into the wire
here is the horn
and the greedy eye. I'm the devil
before you were born
and year into year into year
days of a life, I'm the wind
that whips up the fire
I'm the clothes that poverty wears
I come with an easy hand
play host to your unrest
branding your face with wretchedness
I climb through the windows
and seep under doors
I walk in your shadow
and I paint it black
I'm the load welded to your back.

Kevin's Fortune

A tangled froth of green, no more light than a cave
        I was beating a way through
blistered with a thousand bites, boots twisting on tree roots
        dreaming of a miracle

sopping and wringing and steaming
        and there he stood
up to his waist in water
        'are you looking for a mate?' he said.

♦   ♦   ♦

We made company, Moonlight Beach,
sea lapping at the flaps of our tent
him teaching me: bend, lift, sluice, look.
Festering rats. His love of birds.

Swinging to the beat of a heavy mud-sucked stride
I shared his labours by day
and his blankets by night
– my windfall, my fortune, my trove.

I went foreign and found home, briefly
on this earth, in this life, I found home.

The Gate

Not a farm labourer but should rush from the old doomed country to such a paradise as New Zealand — A GOOD LAND — . . . A LAND OF OIL, OLIVES AND HONEY; — A LAND WHERE IN THOU MAY'ST EAT BREAD WITHOUT SCARCENESS . . . Away then . . . away! New Zealand is the Promised Land for you.

———

The sober truth is, that the ancient world owed its character to the fact that nothing good could take root in it till the different races had it out, till the weak were either massacred or assimilated . . . . The original sin was then, and still is, weakness.

A long time ago there was a gate in the heart of the city. It was an ancient gate. The people behind the gate were called many things. One thing they had in common was their experience of the gate, so I am going to call them the gate people.

The gatekeepers held a meeting to debate the state of the gate; one man presented a plan for a new gate. The gatekeepers were very worried.

Up to this time they had sent gate people back to where they came from. But now the floodgates had opened. People were arriving from all over the world. Everything had got mixed up. There were gate people wandering around the streets amid the ordinary citizens.

The gatekeepers believed this land was their Promised Land. Many ordinary citizens shared this dream. They were the chosen people. Now the hoped-for Promised Land was beginning to look like the nightmare of their old land.

The ancient gate tainted the heart of the city. The walls were not high enough. Citizens did not want to see gate people. Land was losing value; businesses were losing money.

A great deal hung on the new gate. 'Let us not hesitate,' said the men.

And so, the great removal began.

The gate people were escorted down through the streets and taken away. For the new gate had been built at a sacred distance from the city. Over time many people passed through the gate and became gate people; and many of these were never seen or heard from again.

Some citizens pretended that the gate had nothing to do with them. Yet no one, not even the pretenders, could forget that the gate existed.

On the slope above the sea, the wide, high, heavy gate stood. This is a story about the gate, but the land on which the gate stood had its own story.

The spirits of the land lifted. Cracks appeared in the gate, it began to move.

This gate 'must be made to sit still even if we have to chain it down,' said a gatekeeper.

But the spirits of the land continued to lift, rain came, particles shifted and the gate, in the end, was fated to a slow, buckling, twisted decline.

Today we hardly think of the gate at all. Many years have passed since the high, wide, heavy gate stood on the slope above the sea.

People go out to the land and walk in the remnants of the old gate garden and are refreshed by the sea air. Sometimes you will see a visitor standing on the site gazing into the big space the way a migrant might stand on the shore, thinking of their homeland, as if messages were being sent on the waves.

The past is never really passed.

And so it is that the land spirits still stir and lift, burdened yet with the imprint. On days when the mist rolls in over the slope you too may feel the gate in the air above and hear the grinding ache of the hinges as it opens and the gate people come to the threshold.

The Asylum Keys

What happened to the keys? More than a thousand keys
– maybe they were melted down, reborn
like the thistledown, setting out from burnt leaves
all afternoon, migrating

over the site I go, trying another perspective,
coming up from below, narrating the trees
the trees that sound like yesterday;
slogging through mud – scar tissue
torn with every rain,
the undertow drags me in.

Or widening out as if in flight
scrambling through scrub
to reach Mt Charlotte's height, scratched,
ill-humoured – to look down on it all
as if I were God.

Reports, another thesis, papers
– the long, tall voices of academics,
utterly objective; and myself
creeping in at every turn
harvesting details like a detective

biscuit-coloured mortar, brick crumbs
I study them, quartz pebbles

from Shag River – *not near,*
not even close.

The thistledown knows more than I,
up from the land it comes
turning like so many pilgrims
like souls rising, like a clue,
in the silver ships of themselves

the hearts
I can't hear in the wind
beating; the asylum
locking me out – a ghost
from the future
come to haunt the past
– I listen.

Epistle of Mick

I walked the land. there was neither roads nor horse
tracks and not a house in view. from camp to camp all my
possessions about me clanging and banging. nothing but
a noise to myself. then back and not a bit better off than
when I left. slurred my way into the law's arms and they sent
me out here for mending and healing. like the convent at
Clare rooms go deep. one behind the other. invisible lines
not to be crossed. I'm half the man I was Seamus. lost my
shadow on the ship going downhill. is this the summer? is
it our summer or someone else's summer? at home they're
thinking I'm a lucky man. who'd ever believe the world
was made of so much water. nights are filled with restless
tongues. everything smells of cold and old shoes. you can't
have a motion without asking. I carried my cross all the
long distance. I carry it still. my compass. the man upstairs
reading all our writing so I'm giving this letter to an outside
fella as I know he'll put a stamp on it. would you come out
and see me Seamus. a visit would mean the world. haven't
touched a drop in three months. but this is a devil of a place
for getting out of.

Epistle of Kevin

The flood came down like a wall. My man, lost his footing.
That was the last of him. A broken body racked in a heap
of logs. I felt too much. Estranged from the birds and the
trees, in the days after, so alone it hardly mattered what
became of me. Trapped in a cage, conversing with spirits.
Brain fever. The men carried me out to the clipper. I woke
in a house of strangers. They call it asylum. They tell me to
sit and to stand. They tell me to eat. They give me a shovel
and tell me to dig round the edges. Two men in one body
to be corrected, an actor in my own life. The fever does not
rest. Swirling up in my sleep, I stretch out my arm and grab
nothing. Each night he drowns again in me.

The Asylum Songbirds

I

Decorated walls imitate the sun
paintings on the painted walls
invite the viewer
to a rural scene – walking
out the door, walking through a wall
into summer, autumn, winter, the coming
cheerfulness of spring

the seasons wrapped in frames
a liberty that's lost
a confinement that is strange

as songbirds
when first placed inside a cage
fight and flutter
until the spirit's broken in the bird
and what is strange becomes familiar.

II

Brought to heel, stripped, your belongings
locked away – mastering the scripts
what you ought and ought not say – welcome
to the 'forcing house of change'.

III

You move, you talk
inside the room your sounds are human

my name is so and so, you say, my name is
                                        whatever
the doctor, the guard, the attendant
chooses to call me.

IV

In memory of your living
– free to come and go, to have a moment
on your own, to be unseen –

the songbird singing
as it clings against the wire, shifts
from perch to floor, exiled
from the boundless spring
when all birds sing

to find a mate, to make a home.

Second Epistle of Grace

My dearest Una, this is not a letter I could ever have
imagined writing, my dear sister, it is a burden I send. Aidan
left. More than a year passed, no answer came, and I was
in great trouble. He said 'love' he said 'my wife' he said 'this
is our chance to move up in the world'. Then he walked into
a cloud and vanished.

It was a dream. I'd tied my scarf to the wishing tree
praying to the Mother of Good Counsel for a good man.
And there he was, at the crossroads, leading me into
the dance.

Dear sister, it was a dream and I clung to the dream,
searching among the streets and houses. No money, no
work and no word. I could not go forward and I could
not go back. My thoughts became phantoms. I no longer
knew how I was to be.

There was a day of great cold and everything went dark
from that day. Until this. Dearest sister, I have been in the
asylum for months without knowing it.

The Word of Agnes

Dying was something we did in great numbers
children and women dying, men
building a road to nowhere
dying as they did
I come from the land of the hungry

the lords of the land took our land
and living in fear of their fear
sent us as cargo to sea
                the lords with their sums
and their greed, it was cheaper
to lose us than feed us.

My boy was a zero boy
the sole day of his life was a scream
joining the crowds of our people
unresting in the sea.

One man uses you badly and what follows that
is history. Home on the streets
working nights, what would you have us do?
you with your books and your highfalutin talk

you think I'm the rags that I wear
you think I'm the fruit

gone rotten on the tree, you think
you can see the living of our lives

I'm under the cloud of my country
the voices are speaking from the cloud.
I am Agnes. I am many.

Night Descends

It is the late day hour for the birds. They have so many errands
to attend to – this bough to the next bough, sweeping across
the open paddock, circling the canopy. Then back, back into
the thick of it, the shadowy leaf thicket. What they found there,
what they left there, what they have to say about it. Oh, say,
say to the world. It is rush hour for the birds, it is feeding and
homing time. It is all at once singing time

the day quickens its fold

Agnes, believing she could fly through the window,
believing she was only one roof away from Heaven, is
banished to a far hut. Out of harm's way. Agnes, who held
herself so lightly in the world as it is, slips into a world
without tethers. Her world, where she is a prophetess and
each incoming sound – running water, keys clanging against
keys, wheels on gravel – each sound is a private message

dusk blooming, red, to see red, so rare to see red in the land,
a painful shout

the hoe and shovel stand to attention in the shed. Long
hours men bent, re-laying stones, the god of work come
down to earth in a wheelbarrow. Turning his barrow upside
down Thomas moved faster than any of them – here to
there, there to here. The attendant yelling, 'that's not how
it's done, turn your wheelbarrow up the right way!' 'I tried

it that way,' Thomas said, 'and them men over there filled
it full of stones.'

the right way, the wrong way, the way, *away*

one more touch of the sun. Grey moth and dragonfly,
day scent of leaf and flower

the dew all on her breast . . . she whistles and she sings
she goes home in the evening
with the dew all on her wings

Grace moves to the sway of the past, her heart wakes, the
roads waking to the feet of young men and women, the old
people dressed in their best. The feet singing as the fiddler
starts. *Turning about in the air*. A vision in the glass of the day
room – the crossroads dance at dusk

she cannot speak of it. There is no one to listen.

Water blue. Blue of postmarks.
Blue of temperance and sobriety
the shade without balancing the shade within

Mick tunes to the new order. The rambling of his day
becomes a clarity. The chaplain listens in. Mick speaking –
rhythmic, a beautiful tenor – prays to a higher order. God
holds the key. The chaplain cannot account for the sound
of sanity, scratches his head.

Patient files, their unsent letters, locked away, the light of day departing. Surf beats at the cliff, a pulse travels through rock and clay. The laundry takes on the air of a ghost ship, rows of women lie down, their toil vanished into the white sheets – the mangles, the coppers, the tubs, the washing boards, print of their tired hands

What does the night say to the earth as it evens the colours out? Base notes from the gully – click and tap, nudge and push – it is grasshopper, caterpillar, black beetle, it is worm in her corridor

and Agnes, growing smaller and smaller
into a girl of seven
wearing the wood to a hollow
begging with her body to be freed

grief lies down with pain. The songbird
covers its head with its wing. Pain lies down with loneliness.
All lie down with suffering

a restless sleeper tempted from his bed; another
feels under her pillow for the broken rosary

the sun hands over to the moon
embers die in the grate

my home is here, my home
is here – morepork, morepork.
Night.

◆ ◆ ◆

Rekindling the fire
a glassy sea, dew on the lawn – Truby
dresses and shaves. The day
puts on its uniform: order and cleanliness
calm and serenity.

Epilogue

In the dark of sunlight on the leaves
underneath the shedding bark of gums
atmosphere is like a mind in waiting; the weeping
wych-elm sweeping to the ground
flush with summer foliage, chestnut flowers
hum, November's home to bees.

Does the patients' labour linger
blurred beneath the widening reach of green?
Though it sounds like wishful thinking
let their spirits come, redress the doors and locks
by standing in the open. Lives
I cannot enter, all
that the wind secures . . . and trees

– air from every day becoming years
captured in their carbon; the silence
broken by a breath, the heft of mast
and sail – sentinels they seem.
The keepers. The heartwood.

Notes

THE SPEED OF GOD | pages 1–39

3   'Into the Blue Light'. The Kilmog is a hilly area 20 kilometres north of Dunedin. Kaikawaka, also called the New Zealand cedar, stands out in the cloud forest on Leith Saddle, close to the city.

5   'Titipounamu Tapping the Beech Forest'. Titipounamu, the rifleman, New Zealand's smallest bird.

7   'Mackenzie Country'. Pastoral lessees in the Mackenzie Basin apply for 'consent' to the Commissioner of Crown Lands to change the use of the land. This notion of consent has, to date, led to widespread irrigation schemes and intensive dairy farming. The impact on the environment has been brutal.

12 'Normanby'. South Canterbury.

13 '10th April 1968'. The date ex-tropical Cyclone Giselle hit New Zealand and the interisland ferry *Wahine* sank in Wellington Harbour with the loss of fifty-one lives. The storm caused devastation across the country.

15 'Kōtukutuku'. Tree fuchsia.

17 'Kāhu'. Harrier hawk.

Seacliff Lunatic Asylum (later Seacliff Mental Hospital) was north of Dunedin, about halfway to Palmerston, in an isolated coastal spot within a forested reserve.

Opened in 1884 at a cost of £78,000, which was a very large amount for the times (in today's terms approximately NZ$15 million), Seacliff provided housing for five hundred patients and fifty staff. For fifty years it was New Zealand's largest public building. The architect, R. A. Lawson, invested a great deal in the external impact of the asylum. The effect of the design and magnitude of the building, with its 160-foot (50-metre) surveillance tower, was authoritative, imposing and no doubt fear-inducing. The building was however on unstable land which led to many subsequent difficulties – perhaps that is a metaphor for the whole institution.

Dunedin's population had been growing rapidly. Its first such institution, the Littlebourne Mental Asylum, built in 1863 and located in the centre of the city, had been designed to accommodate twenty-one 'inmates', but ten years later the asylum held 230 people. The overcrowding prompted the building of Seacliff, out of range of civic life.

A major factor in the population growth had been Julius Vogel's mass assisted immigration programme. Many of the new arrivals did not have the resources or the support that would have enabled them to adapt easily to life in New Zealand. Married women were deserted by husbands, single men self-medicated with alcohol, single women employed as domestic servants were expected to manage and run every aspect of a household and were often subject to sexual predation.

The Irish proportion of Otago immigrants rose rapidly, doubling the Irish-born population in New Zealand. Not all were prepared for colonial life. The Irish famine was in living memory; and many had travelled on their own, leaving family and tight-knit communities. Discrimination, poverty and isolation compounded their difficulties. Irish Catholics became one of the groups overrepresented in the asylum population.

The Lunatics Act 1882 had a broad legal definition, rather than a medical diagnosis, of what constituted a lunatic. The term was applied indiscriminately to all those who, for whatever reason, were deemed incapable of managing themselves or their affairs. Anyone regarded as socially or economically problematic, including vagrants and those working the streets, could be held under the act.

Once committed to the asylum it was difficult to get out, having been defined as 'insane' making it almost impossible for a person to defend themself as sane since they were no longer judged a trustworthy witness of their own experience; their fate lay in the hands of the authorities. Those with a family willing to vouch for them, provide support and take responsibility for their immediate aftercare received more sympathetic treatment.

In many ways the experience was more akin to a prison than a hospital and the certified insane had no legal rights. The asylum experience tended to have a corrosive effect on identity, especially for those inappropriately incarcerated. Those in the institution for longer than a year were likely to stay for a very long time. Many never entered society again: 'half the patients in the Dunedin and Seacliff asylum database died in an asylum in New Zealand' (McCarthy, *Migration, Ethnicity, and Madness*, p. 203).

Dr Duncan MacGregor was appointed inspector of the Dunedin Lunatic Asylum in 1873; between 1876 and 1882 he served as the asylum's medical officer. In 1886 he was appointed to the national positions of inspector of lunatic asylums and inspector of hospitals and charitable institutions. Influenced by Social

Darwinian ideas, he feared New Zealand was being overrun by a flood of immigrants from lowly backgrounds. He was the greatest mentor and ally of Dr Truby King, who became the medical superintendent of Seacliff in 1889. King stayed thirty years, before moving on to focus on child welfare, having already founded the Plunket Society in 1907.

The hospital functions of Seacliff were closed in 1973, and the original building site became the Truby King Recreation Reserve with the last remaining building in the reserve demolished in 1992.

43   'Epistle of Maeve'. Letter from Maeve McCrea to Deirdre Boyle.

44   'First Epistle of Grace'. Letter from Grace Dolan (Ireland) to Aidan Dolan (NZ).

50   'A Great Many Never Seen a Ship Before'. Alice Gilmore (Auckland) to her brother and sister (Ards Peninsula, Down), in McCarthy, *Irish Migrants in New Zealand*, pp. 110–11. Some spellings have been changed from the original.

54   'The Workhouse Girls'. I am indebted to Ciara Breathnach and her paper, 'Even "Wilder Workhouse Girls"', which was a key source for this work. Agnes, Maeve McCrea and Deirdre Boyle, their stories and their voices, were partly inspired by Ciara Breathnach's paper together with newspaper reports from the time.

60   'Kevin's Fortune'. Coal Island.

61   'The Gate'. Opening quotations. *Labourers' Union Chronicle*, 29 November 1873, p. 1, as quoted in Phillips, 'History of Immigration'; MacGregor, 'The Problem of Poverty in New Zealand'.

66   'Epistle of Mick'. Letter from Mick Pearse (Seacliff) to Seamus Ryley (Dunedin).

67 'Epistle of Kevin'. Writing to himself.

68 'The Asylum Songbirds'. 'Obviously many institutions, such as the band and library already described, should be regarded in the light of elevating, refining and soothing influences. In addition may be named the painting of the building throughout in light pleasant colours . . . polishing the floors, decorating rooms and corridors with pictures, flowers, and ferns, and the introduction of singing-birds.' Truby King in Tod, *Seacliff*, p. 41.

70 'Second Epistle of Grace'. Letter from Grace Dolan (Seacliff) to her sister Una O'Toole (Ireland).

73 'Night Descends'. The portrait of Thomas is based on a true account, see McLaglan, *Stethoscope and Saddlebags*.

74 '*The dew all on her breast . . .*'. From 'The Lark in the Morning', a folk song.

77 'Epilogue'. Truby King Recreation Reserve.

Sources

Braham, Peter, *Closing the Asylum: The Mentally Ill in Society*, Harmondsworth, Penguin, 1995.

Breathnach, Ciara, 'Even "Wilder Workhouse Girls": The Problem of Institutionalisation among Irish Immigrants to New Zealand 1874', *Journal of Imperial and Commonwealth History*, vol. 39, issue 5, 2011.

Brookes, Barbara and Jane Thomson, eds, *'Unfortunate Folk': Essays on Mental Health Treatment, 1863–1992*, Dunedin, Otago University Press, 2001.

Chapman, Lloyd, *In a Strange Garden: The Life and Times of Truby King*, Auckland, Penguin, 2003.

Glassey, Phil, David Barrell and Belinda Smith Lyttle, *The Hazard Significance of Landslides in and around Dunedin City*, GNS Science Consultancy Report 2013/339, 2014.

McCarthy, Angela, *Irish Migrants in New Zealand, 1840–1937: 'The Desired Haven'*, Woodbridge, Suffolk, Boydell Press, 2005.

McCarthy, Angela, *Migration, Ethnicity, and Madness: New Zealand, 1860–1910*, Dunedin, Otago University Press, 2015.

MacGregor, Duncan, 'The Problem of Poverty in New Zealand', *NZ Magazine*, July 1876.

McLaglan, Eleanor S. Baker, *Stethoscope and Saddlebags: An Autobiography*, Auckland, Collins, 1965.

Olssen, Erik, *A History of Otago*, Dunedin, McIndoe, 1984.

Phillips, Jock, 'History of Immigration – The Great Migration: 1871 to 1885', Te Ara – the Encyclopedia of New Zealand, www.teara.govt.nz/en/history-of-immigration/page-8

Tod, Frank, *Seacliff: A History of the District to 1970* [Dunedin, Otago Daily Times Print, 1971].

Acknowledgements

Thank you to the editors of the following publications in which some of the poems, or versions of them, have appeared: *Landfall*, *Otago Daily Times*, *takahē*, *Poetry New Zealand*, *JAAM*, *New Zealand Poet Laureate blog*, *Stand Magazine*, *The Rialto*, *Shot Glass Journal* and *Manifesto Aotearoa: 101 Political Poems* (edited by Philip Temple and Emma Neale).

Thank you also to Creative New Zealand for a Quick Response Grant received in 2017. I am immensely grateful to the Robert Burns Fellowship Selection Committee for awarding me the fellowship in 2018.

My heartfelt thanks to my dedicatees Jane Duran and Alison Rutherford, and also Alison Glenny, for reading and considering the poems at various times, to Vincent O'Sullivan for his kindness and good craic. Very little would have been possible without the love and support of friends and family; my thanks to Lynley Edmeades, Laurence Fearnley, Bernadette Hall, Maia Mistral and Kate Vercoe; my brothers Patrick and Daniel Gallagher; Tracy Gallagher, Ella, Josh and Molly. Abiding love and thanks to Sonja Mitchell.